M000250122

MOTOR COACHES AND CHARABANCS

James Taylor

SHIRE PUBLICATIONS
Bloomsbury Publishing Plc
PO Box 883, Oxford, OX1 9PL, UK
1385 Broadway, 5th Floor, New York, NY 10018,
USA

E-mail: shire@bloomsbury.com
www.shirebooks.co.uk

SHIRE is a trademark of Osprey Publishing Ltd

First published in Great Britain in 2020

A catalogue record for this book is available from the
British Library.

ISBN: PB 978 1 78442 412 1
       eBook 978 1 78442 413 8
       ePDF 978 1 78442 410 7
       XML 978 1 78442 411 4

20 21 22 23 24   10 9 8 7 6 5 4 3 2 1

Typeset by PDQ Digital Media Solutions, Bungay, UK

Printed and bound in India by Replika Press Private Ltd.

COVER IMAGE
Front cover: 1950 Bedford OB Duple Vista Coach
at Sumburgh Head in Scotland (Alamy). Back cover:
Decal and logo from Royal Blue coach 1299 (OTT
98), built in 1953 (Barry Skeates/CC BY 2.0).

TITLE PAGE IMAGE

When the earliest underfloor engined chassis became
available in the late 1940s, they brought with them
full front coachwork. As a result, new bodies fitted
on older chassis that had survived the war years
followed suit. This was one of 30 integral construction
(chassisless) rebuilds by Beadle for Southdown, using
pre-war Leyland Tiger TS8 running units.

CONTENTS PAGE IMAGE
This 1973 AEC Reliance wears the distinctive livery
of Yelloway Motor Services, which retained its
independence as other operators grouped together.
(see page 39)

ACKNOWLEDGEMENTS
Images are acknowledged as follows:

Alamy, pages 11, 20 -21, 30 (top), 37 (top), 46, 47 (top),
48, 53, 54, 60 (bottom), 61 (bottom); Alan Farrow/
Public Domain, pages 9, 16 (both), 25; Andrew Bone/
CC BY 2.0, page 29 (top); Arriva436/CC BY SA 3.0,
pages 1, 49 (bottom), 59 (bottom); author's collection,
pages 4, 6, 13, 27, 28, 30, 35, 36, 37 (bottom), 38,
39, 42, 44, 45 (bottom), 47 (bottom), 50; calflier001/
CC BY-SA 2.0, page 58; Caravans and Charabancs/
CC BY-ND 2.0, pages 7, 8, 10; Charles01/CC BY-SA
3.0, page 57 (top); Chris Sampson/CC BY 2.0, pages
40 -41, 51 (top); citytransportinfo/CC BY 2.0, page 31;
Editor5807/CC BY 3.0, page 22; FCox143, page 62;
Felix O/CC BY-SA 3.0, page 49 (top); Geof Sheppard/
CC BY-SA 3.0, pages 30 (bottom), 34 (bottom), 45
(top); Geof Sheppard/CC BY SA 4.0, pages 18 and 24;
Jon's pics/CC BY SA 2.0, pages 12 (bottom left), 19;
Kk70088/CC BY-SA 4.0, page 61 (top); Martin 49/CC
BY 2.0, page 29 (bottom); Mattforbes/CC BY-SA 3.0,
page 59 (top); Paul Williams, page 43; Phil Sangwell/
CC BY 2.0, page 60 (top); RXUYDC/Public Domain,
page 57 (bottom); RXUYDC/CC BY-SA 3.0, pages
33, 55; Secret Coach Park/CC BY-SA 2.0, pages 3 and
56; Sludge G/CC BY-SA 2.0, page 51 (bottom); Steve
Glover/CC BY 2.0, pages 12 (bottom right) and 34
(top); The Bus Archive, page 14; Tony Hisgett/CC BY
2.0, page 17.

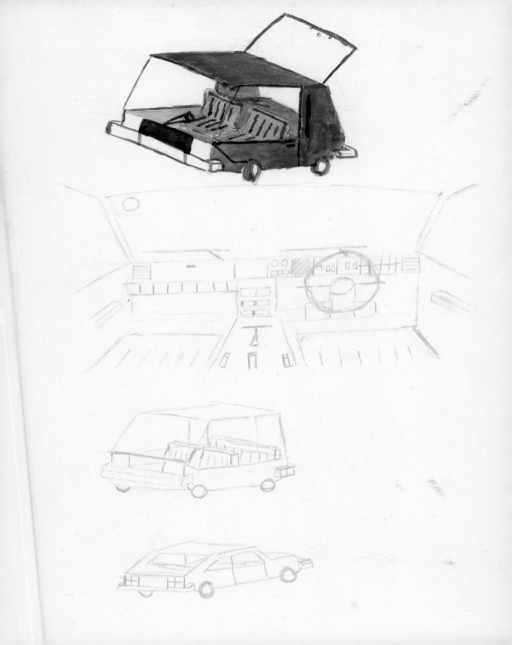

Hove

31495

25 Raphael Road

Hove 3

Sussex

CONTENTS

TIMPSON'S
SILVER CHARABANCS

De Luxe Type Motor Coaches

FOR

Annual Outings, Beanfeasts, Private Pleasure Parties,

ETC.

One of the largest and finest fleet of Motor Coaches in the South of England, capable of —— carrying up to 600 in one party. ——

Timpson's Chief Office, Garage and Works :—

175 RUSHEY GREEN, CATFORD,
S.E. 6.

Telephone : Lee Green 1818.

FROM CHARABANC TO EXPRESS COACH

MODERN COACH SERVICES have their origins in the nineteenth century, and in particular in the factory outings that were organised during holiday periods in the industrial towns of northern England and the Midlands. These holidays grew out of an ancient tradition of celebrating the saint's day of the local church, and local councils often extended this into a full week's holiday. Such holiday periods were known in the north as 'wakes weeks', and rapidly shed their religious connections to become entirely secular in nature.

Holidays in those days were unpaid, of course; paid holidays would not become the norm until the late 1930s. Typically, the local factories and mills closed down once a year for a week, allowing maintenance to be carried out on the machinery. In Lancashire, the major towns took their holiday on a different week during the summer so that from June to September one town was on holiday each week. This tradition disappeared during the twentieth century with the gradual establishment of a common school holiday period across England – but there remain traces of it in places such as the car factories of the Midlands, where the annual works closure in the summer allows production staff to refit manufacturing areas and assembly lines for the new models to be announced in the autumn.

By the late nineteenth century, it had also become the tradition for the workers in a particular town or factory to band together for a special day out during that holiday week.

OPPOSITE
This timetable for Timpson's Silver Charabancs dates from summer 1921 and lists daily services from London to Hastings, Sunday services to Margate, and half-day trips to such places as Tunbridge Wells, Dorking and Maidstone, as well as trips to race meetings within a 100-mile radius of London.

Some of the more enlightened factory owners actually organised an annual works outing for them and contributed to the costs. These works outings might be to the country, to major horse-racing events, or to the seaside, and transport was arranged in convoys of open-topped horse-drawn vehicles that were known as charabancs. Other outings would be organised by working men's clubs, and would be funded by the participants themselves. The costs were such that the men were most unlikely to be accompanied by wives and families, and the day out was just as likely to become a pub crawl as a genuine visit to a place of interest!

The word 'charabanc' is French in origin (*char à bancs*), and translates as 'carriage with wooden benches'. The charabanc originated in France in the 1840s as a sporting vehicle, used at race meetings or for hunting or shooting parties. Enlarged to suit the greater numbers to be carried on a works outing, a charabanc might consist of several rows of forward-facing seats, perhaps with a removable fabric roof to give some protection against the inclement weather of a typical British summer's day.

When motor vehicles began to proliferate at the start of the twentieth century, and motor buses entered the picture, the development of the motorised charabanc was inevitable.

The archetypal charabanc is represented in this picture, which probably dates from c.1920, the year when the vehicle was registered. The coachwork is open, with a pram-type folding hood stowed at the rear, and each full-width row of seats has its own entrance door on each side of the body.

This smaller than average charabanc is based on an ex-military Fiat 15TER lorry chassis. The number displayed on the running-board identifies the party of charabanc trippers, enabling the photographer to supply the correct photograph afterwards.

Motor charabancs began to appear around 1910; it was in 1911 that W.C. Standerwick of Blackpool bought their first motor charabanc, a Karrier (built in Huddersfield) with chain drive to the rear axle and headlamps lit by oil. In the south of England, Royal Blue of Bournemouth acquired their first charabancs in 1913. Both companies had earlier operated horse-drawn vehicles, and these purchases were a natural progression for them. After 1914, the demand for motor lorries to assist the British Army fighting in Belgium and France would lead to worthwhile developments that would eventually cross over to charabancs as well.

The open-top charabanc was a very basic vehicle and its wooden bench seats were uncomfortable, but its shortcomings could be forgotten in the atmosphere of excitement, camaraderie and adventure that typically accompanied a works outing. For many people, these annual outings were their only chance to escape from the grim environment of an industrial city. A posed photograph of the party aboard their charabanc might be a highlight of the trip and, for those who could afford a copy, a treasured memory of it. To protect rain from dampening this enthusiasm, charabanc bodies had a large and heavy folding hood stowed at the rear. It was traditional for the

WHITEGATE, LAUNDRY ANNUAL TRIP

The inscription on the picture identifies this as the Whitegate Laundry Annual Trip, which in this case was probably pictured before its departure from Blackpool. The vehicle is probably another former military lorry – in this case a Daimler Y Type.

men of the party to assist with erecting this when it became necessary. These hoods had windows made of flexible mica – which did allow a view out, but became discoloured and opaque over time and were quite easily torn.

These early motor charabancs were also not entirely reliable, and more than one works outing must have been spoiled for the participants by a mechanical breakdown. It is not hard to imagine the men in the party showing off whatever mechanical knowledge they had by trying to help the driver to get everything running smoothly again. Nor is it hard to imagine them being called upon to push the ailing vehicle to a place of safety while the womenfolk stood by to reduce the weight – quite probably in the pouring rain.

Early motor charabanc excursions were always an adventure, especially if they involved long distances, and Peter and Judith A. Deegan (in *Standerwick & Scout*) tell the story of a pioneering week-long excursion to London run by the Standerwick brothers of Blackpool at the close of the 1912 season, in October. 'Owing to insufficient knowledge of locations where petrol might be obtained, they lashed sufficient petrol cans to the running boards to ensure their return to Blackpool!' The excursion was considered such a major event that after their safe return to Blackpool the passengers presented the charabanc's driver, Vic Standerwick (brother of Walter, whose initials the company bore), with a commemorative gold watch.

Some charabanc operators remained in business during the First World War, and by the end of the decade they were joined by many others. Many newly demobbed servicemen had learned to drive during their enforced service in the Army, and they resolved to put their skill to good use during peacetime. There were plenty of military lorries available that were now surplus to requirements and available for good prices, and these often formed the basis of a one-man charabanc business.

The business model seems to have been repeated over and over again around the country, although inevitably only a proportion of these small charabanc operations survived while others went to the wall. Typically, an ex-military lorry might earn its keep as an open wagon or a van doing road haulage work over the winter months. Come the better weather, the lorry body would be removed, and in its place would be fitted a charabanc body. The owner would then earn revenue from excursion work over the summer months, replacing the lorry body at the end of the season and going back into the haulage business.

Even though the charabancs of the immediate post-war period rode on solid tyres and were typically unable to exceed 12mph with a full load of passengers, long-distance tours and excursions gradually became popular. By 1921, for example, five-day tours from Yorkshire to London were being advertised. The charabanc became a common sight, and there are several references to it in the literature of the time. A warm

The obligatory charabanc trip photograph was taken here at the Chelmsford Brewery. There are women and children on this one, which departed from Thurrock. The vehicle is a solid-tyred AEC, and the picture dates from around 1920.

Registered to J&G Smith of Douglas, Isle of Man, this is a ten passenger Ford TT charabanc wearing early pneumatic tyres. The photographer's number on the running-board again helps to identify the photograph for would-be purchasers. The picture dates from April 1922.

and enjoyable reminiscence of a men's charabanc outing that became a glorified pub crawl is included in *A Story* by Dylan Thomas (written for a BBC radio broadcast in 1953 and also known as *The Outing*). Here, the vehicle is referred to as a 'chara', which was a common popular abbreviation that derived from the British pronunciation of 'sharrabang' – an approximation of the French original.

There was little difference between chassis intended for goods work and chassis intended to carry passengers in the years immediately after the First World War, and as a result the passengers in a charabanc tended to sit quite high off the ground. This made these vehicles more than a little top-heavy, especially if they were overloaded (and the temptation to earn more revenue by carrying more than the planned number of passengers must have been great). There were some reports of charabancs that overturned on the steep and winding roads leading to popular coastal villages, and with no real protection for the passengers some of these accidents resulted in fatalities.

This was one factor that led to the demise of the charabanc. Another was that by the mid-1920s dedicated bus chassis were also becoming available, and offered higher standards of comfort and safety. So the charabanc largely disappeared during this decade, even though a few remained in use for many more years as novelties for the summer season and to fuel nostalgia.

Meanwhile, the 1920s saw a massive expansion in the demand for excursions and tours. The coach operators were not slow to respond, and the fleets of the most successful among them grew much larger. In 1921, Timpson's Silver Charabancs, a south London firm, claimed to own 'one of the largest and finest fleets of motor coaches in the south of England' which was 'capable of carrying up to 600 in one party'. As the typical charabanc of the time carried somewhere around 30 passengers, that implied a fleet of around 20 coaches. Two years later, the Timpson's fleet consisted of around 45 vehicles. There were early examples of the package holiday, too: by summer 1927, Timpson's (the Silver Charabancs name had been dropped by this point) were offering a six-day holiday to Ilfracombe and North Devon for just under £10 a head, all hotels included. There were weekly departures from the company's coach station in a former tram depot at Catford, south-east London.

However, much more important was that the 1920s also saw some major changes in the type of coach services being provided, as many charabanc operators expanded their horizons. In late September 1919, for example, Royal Blue of Bournemouth took advantage of a rail strike and used their vehicles to run a coach service from Bournemouth to London. Strike over, they capitalised on the success of their venture; in 1920 they ran the service twice a week, but a year later the frequency had multiplied to twice a day.

Timpson's established a twice-daily summer service between London and Hastings in 1919, and over the next few

The Royal Red Coach Company was founded in Llandudno in 1907 to pioneer motor coach tours, and initially ran 15-seater Dennis charabancs. This picture of the company's later 30-seat charabancs, still on solid tyres, was taken at the Sychnant Pass in Conwy, much of which lies within the Snowdonia National Park.

years developed a number of other regular south coast services. By 1922 they were running daily summer services to Brighton and Margate, too, plus excursions to other coastal destinations and to racecourses and inland sightseeing areas. The return fare to Margate was £1 – by no means cheap, as Tom McLachlan points out in *Grey-Green and Contemporaries*, when £200 a year was well above average earnings. Then, on 11 February 1925, Greyhound Motors established a scheduled service between London and Bristol that was the first of its kind, carrying passengers not only from one city to the other but also picking up and setting down at various points between them.

These changes in the demand being placed on motor coaches led inevitably to design changes as well. The move away from charabanc bodies had begun in the early 1920s, and by about 1925 the pure charabanc was something of an anachronism – although many remained in service. For touring work, all-weather bodies became popular; these typically had fixed side windows and perhaps fixed front and rear domes, with a large fabric 'sunshine roof' between them that could be opened to let in the best of the weather. Most importantly, they were far easier to convert to closed configuration if that weather deteriorated.

The third option in the early 1920s was the fully enclosed saloon body, and this gained ground rapidly as long-distance express services became more common. Many of them had a stowage rack built into the rear of the roof to carry passengers'

luggage. The design of both these and the all-weather bodies reflected dissatisfaction with charabanc-style seating, with its rows of seats that ran the full width of the vehicle and were each accessed by separate doors. In its place came the saloon style, typically with pairs of seats on either side of a central gangway, and a single access door to the passenger saloon.

Timpson's boasted on the leaflet for their 1929 Spring Programme: 'All coaches are constructed with a clear centre gangway and fitted with pneumatic tyres.' This, too, was a change driven by demand. The solid tyres typical of early charabancs delivered a bone-jarring ride, which was completely at odds with the idea of luxury travel that had gained a hold in the coaching business. Pneumatic tyres not only cushioned the occupants of the vehicle against the worst road shocks but also helped to make higher road speeds feasible.

Changing times: this flyer for Timpson's Spring 1929 Programme carries a picture of one of the company's latest coaches. No longer a charabanc, it is an all-weather type.

If the early 1920s had seen a rapid expansion of the whole coaching industry, the latter half of the decade became a period of intense competition. Quite apart from the new start-ups, some of the established service bus companies entered the market with their own express coach services. Crosville (operating in north- and mid-Wales and in north-west England), Midland Red (whose services radiated out from Edgbaston) and Red & White (who covered Gloucestershire and south-east Wales) were the main operators to do so. By 1930, there were no fewer than 18 different companies that ran coaches between London and Oxford, and coach design had changed for ever. Long-distance travel by coach gradually became less of an adventure and more of a realistic alternative to the railways – and that, in turn, persuaded several railway companies to take an interest in the coaching business.

Get fit and Keep fit

TRAVEL BY

Timpson's

CATFORD
LONDON, S.E.6.

EXD 364

1939
SUMMER SEASON
PROGRAMME

LUXURY TRAVEL: THE 1930s

THE 1930S WITNESSED a major expansion in long-distance express coach services. Although day excursions and half-day mystery tours remained popular, more modern coach designs created the greater reliability that underpinned this expansion.

Right at the start of the decade, the Road Traffic Act of 1930 introduced a national system to regulate passenger road transport, requiring operators to meet certain standards and to apply to regional commissioners before starting new services. A Road Service Licence was required for all express services, excursions and tours, as well as for ordinary stage-carriage services, although private hire work was exempt. The new Act also limited maximum speeds by law to 30mph at all times. One of its effects was to squeeze some of the smaller operators out of business, or to persuade them to seek shelter with one of the two big groups – the Tilling Group and the British Electric Traction group. Meanwhile, some of the larger operators reached agreement with competitors to share services and pool revenues.

London's new Green Line division also started up in 1930, established by the London General Omnibus Company to operate services between the capital and outlying towns within a radius of 30 miles. Green Line used coaches, but there was no need to pre-book a seat and their 'express' services were really limited-stop stage carriage services. Elsewhere, Midland Red opened a similar network but used ordinary single-deck

OPPOSITE
This summer season brochure was produced by Timpson's of Catford in London. The cover shows what was clearly intended to be a Harrington coach body with the famous dorsal fin... (see page 24)

Typical of the way coaches looked by the early 1930s is this AEC Reliance with a body by Clark & Co. of Scunthorpe. There were entrance doors front and rear – but only on the kerb side – and the chassis had a forward-control layout with the driver alongside the engine.

buses for the job. These long-distance services were often in competition with the railway companies, who fought hard to defend their corner when new service applications came before the commissioners. However, as the coach operators were able to price their services more keenly and to run them more frequently, public demand won the day.

The early 1930s also saw the establishment of the first dedicated coach stations, which provided undercover boarding for passengers away from the traffic and bustle of the streets. The very first was established in 1931 by Black & White Motorways at Cheltenham in the large grounds of a Georgian house. By 1934, it had become the hub of express services

An early-1930s Leyland Cub coach owned by Hoyle's of Haslingden in Lancashire. The Cub was also available as a lorry chassis. This small coach has a single entrance door; there is a luggage rack on the rear roof; and the windowed panel on the kerb side of the engine was clearly an attempt to add an attractive feature.

Pictured in much more recent times, the Art Deco façade of London's Victoria Coach Station dates back to the 1930s. This was one of the first proper coach stations to be constructed, and was still functional in its original role in the early twenty-first century.

with a nationwide reach operated by the consortium of six operators known as Associated Motorways. In 1932, another consortium of operators, London Coastal Coaches, opened a dedicated coach station at Victoria in London. With striking administrative buildings in a modern Art Deco style, this soon became the London terminus for most regular coach services. It remains so today.

Even though this was a decade when unemployment was high and the effects of the Great Depression were still being felt, there was a new trend for the middle-aged middle classes to go on extended coach tours to areas such as Cornwall or the Lake District. Operators typically advertised tours and excursions in the local newspapers and on boards outside their own booking offices, and the major London coaching firms – Banfield's, Grey-Green, Timpson's and others – took pre-bookings during normal weekday working hours. Business was boosted even further when the Holidays with Pay Act was passed in 1938, because the numbers of those who could afford holiday coach services or excursions was multiplied by a factor of more than seven.

This was also a period when coach tours to the European continent developed in the wake of new horizons opened up by air travel. Although continental tours were expensive and therefore available only to the comfortably off middle classes (the upper classes were more likely to use their own cars), they became a popular holiday option. Most famous of the operators was probably Motorways Ltd, a company based in London's Haymarket that had entered the business as early as 1920 with a coach service from London to the Mediterranean. Using the slogan, 'see Europe from an armchair', Motorways ran European tours that lasted for up to 32 days – and back home they also operated coach tours of Britain specifically aimed at overseas visitors.

These changes in the coaching business led to changes in the types of coaches that were ordered. Although many older ones remained in service well into the 1930s, the predominant taste was for closed bodies that gave proper protection against the weather. The older Chevrolets and Lancias that had formed the backbone of many small fleets, and the ex-RAF Crossleys that had started life as lorries, gradually disappeared from front-line coach services. In their place came more modern, more reliable types that had been specifically designed for coaching. Yet distance still played an important part in what

This beautifully preserved 1934 AEC Regal was bought second-hand by W.C. Standerwick Ltd of Blackpool in 1937 and, as the signwriting demonstrates, was used on the company's long-distance Blackpool to London service. The 32-seat coach body was built by Beadle in Dartford, Kent.

was and was not possible for coach operators. That 30mph legal limit put restrictions on how far a day tour could go from its departure point.

New designs of coach chassis were already in place by the time the decade opened, and domestic British manufacturers gradually reclaimed the market for themselves. In 1927 Leyland had introduced its new Tiger, with a drop-frame chassis that allowed a much lower build than earlier chassis shared with lorries; two years later AEC introduced its rival Regal, having poached Leyland's chief designer, John Rackham, to design it. These were very much more advanced designs than those that had preceded them, capturing best practice from around the world and blending it into a harmonious and successful whole. The new and lower chassis frames inspired sleeker and more modern-looking bodies, too, and the best of these were designed with quite graceful lines that had an elegance of their own.

Operators who wanted a smaller coach favoured chassis like the Dennis Dart, seen here as a 1933 model with 20-seat coach body by Duple. The body styling swoops typical of that coachbuilder in the 1930s are in evidence here. This coach has also been preserved.

Another popular small coach chassis of the 1930s was the Bedford WLB, which is seen here as a 1935 example. The 20-seat coach body is again by Duple.

CMG 30

HCVC   1935
BEDFORD   WLB

The major suppliers of coach chassis in this period were AEC and Leyland, the former developing its Regal series through the decade while the latter developed its Tiger series. Both types were suitable for either bus or coach bodywork, the coach versions of the chassis usually having an extended rear overhang to support the luggage boot needed for touring work. AEC and Leyland certainly did not have the market to themselves, however. There were popular coach chassis from the likes of Bristol, Commer, Dennis, Gilford, Thornycroft and Tilling-Stevens, while imports from Dodge, Reo and Opel all found buyers. Favourites with the smaller coach operators were cheap and reliable normal-control Bedfords, such as the WTB introduced in 1935 that was designed to seat 26 passengers. Although diesel engines were becoming increasingly popular for stage carriage services on account of their greater economy, coach chassis generally retained petrol engines until the end of the decade, because their quieter running was more acceptable on long journeys and was considered more appropriate to luxury travel.

Bedford followed the WLB with the WTB model in 1935, and the majority were bodied by Duple in one of several styles. This 25-seat coach survives today and is used for passenger services on the Isle of Wight by John Woodhams Vintage Tours of Ryde.

Luxury certainly became the name of the game. For touring and excursion work, operators usually ordered well-equipped bodies with plenty of legroom; Brighton-based Southdown Motor Services, for example, bought six Leyland Tigress coaches in 1936 that seated only 20 in their Burlingham coach bodies, which might otherwise have seated 26. Seats were comfortably upholstered, and interior design generally had an air of luxury that was entirely in keeping with the leisure activities for which many coaches were used. Coach bodies invariably had doors to close off their entrances and prevent draughts, and operators took a pride in how their vehicles were turned out, ensuring they were spotlessly clean and polished at the start of a day's work. On the negative side, heating was generally rudimentary: at best, there would be a circular Clayton radiator-type heater at the front of the passenger saloon, fed by hot water from the engine's cooling system but singularly ineffective at warming anybody sitting more than about two rows of seats behind it.

Coach driving became a respectable and well-paid job. The more professional operators insisted that their drivers were smartly turned out and wore a uniform, which might consist of no more than a peaked cap with an appropriate badge and a white coat worn over otherwise ordinary clothes. During the 1930s, the coach driver became not just the man who drove the vehicle and was responsible for its day-to-day maintenance needs while away from base, but also the tour guide and passengers' friend and confidant. In some circumstances, when consistent with safety, he might lead or at least join in the singalongs that became a feature of tours, excursions and private hire outings to keep the passengers entertained on the less interesting sections of the journey.

Bodywork came from a large number of body makers, both large and small. Many catered only for their local area and were little known further afield, but there were others

... and here is that fin in the metal, on a preserved 1939 Leyland Cheetah. The curves of the Harrington body are complemented by curved cant-rail glass, which offered both a superb view and a light and airy feel to the interior.

whose products were purchased nationwide. A handful of coach body builders stood above the rest. Among them were Harrington (at Hove in Sussex), who built high-quality bodies that incorporated very pleasing lines, recognisably inspired by the Art Deco fashion of the time and by the vogue for streamlining. Duple (based at Hendon in London) were less deliberately distinctive and built in a variety of styles, but forged a strong relationship with Bedford that ensured they were represented at the lower end of the market as well as at the top. Although both Harrington and Duple designs were to a large extent standardised, the colourful liveries that many operators chose helped to introduce a degree of individuality – and there were of course multiple detail options.

Body side decoration was regularly used to soften the lines of coaches and to help distinguish them from single-deck service buses. Flashes in contrasting colour were widespread, with swoops of chrome as well. Harrington bodies were noted for a central 'dorsal fin' above the rearmost window, which acted as a ventilation outlet. Windows might have drop-glasses with louvres above them to prevent draughts, and some coaches even had curtains at the side windows. Many, both large and small, had roof-mounted racks or closed compartments for additional luggage.

The 1930s also witnessed a vogue for streamlining, supposedly based on sound aerodynamic principles borrowed from the aircraft industry but in reality little more than a fashionable nod in that direction. There were a few bizarre results, but mostly coach body builders settled for sloping front ends, often disguising the typical half-cab design with a modesty panel on the nearside and sometimes going as far as a genuine full-width front.

Despite the new preference for closed bodies, people still wanted open-air motoring in the summer, and so in the mid-1930s some coach bodies were still being built with 'sunshine' roofs – fabric sections which opened up a large part of the roof panel in an otherwise closed body to let in fresh air as the coach bowled along. These had a tendency to jam in the open position, and sometimes jammed closed as well, and so some of the more expensive body makers started to use sliding metal panels that were rather more reliable.

The Second World War prolonged the lives of some 1930s coaches. This Leyland Tiger TS2, operated by Southdown Motor Services of Brighton, was re-bodied as a 32-seat coach by Park Royal in 1935, rebuilt again by Portsmouth Aviation in 1948, and is pictured here, still in service and looking smart, in the early 1950s.

Open charabanc and all-weather bodies had allowed little scope for interior embellishment, but the closed bodies of the 1930s allowed designers much freer rein. Recognising that they had to compete with Pullman coaches on the railways and with the high-quality features and fittings of airlines such as Imperial Airways, coach operators began to call for very high levels of interior appointment. Clocks, picnic tables on the seat-backs, polished and even figured or inlaid wood, curtains, ashtrays and flower vases (with fresh flowers daily) became commonplace on coaches. Although there were differing opinions on the most appropriate seat coverings, moquette (a woven fabric) became very popular because it was warmer and more inviting than the usual leather alternative. Its disadvantages were that it needed more regular cleaning, and was more readily damaged.

Some coach operators specified a toilet compartment for coaches used on long-distance services, but others preferred the traditional solution of a comfort stop – usually with refreshments available at a roadside café as well – every two hours or so. The earliest coaches with toilet compartments had actually appeared in 1927, and these compartments were usually equipped with a wash basin, a grab handle (the ride was not always smooth) and towels.

In an effort to offer something new and different, some coach operators experimented with unusual designs or novel interior fittings. This period saw the rise of the so-called Observation Coach which, like the American railway coaches of the same name, offered a raised section that allowed a better view for a few passengers. These often had a 'one-and-a-half-deck' design, with the raised section covering the rear half or rear third of the coach and leaving a large area underneath that could be used for luggage stowage. Some had more quirky designs, with a raised section in the middle. Such interesting designs mostly failed to survive into the post-war era of the late 1940s, however.

WARTIME AND AUSTERITY: THE 1940s AND 1950s

THE OUTBREAK OF war in 1939 put a stop to coach manufacture, as chassis and body makers alike were required to devote their efforts to war matériel for the duration. Coach operators struggled on as best they could until 1942 when they too were required to suspend operations in order to conserve fuel. It was 1946 before services resumed – and the slow pace of national recovery ensured that times would be hard for a few more years.

The war also curtailed coaching activities in a more direct fashion. Although express services continued for a while, the military authorities began to visit operators to requisition vehicles for war service. Some were used as troop transports or as ambulances, and very few returned to service

As the coach industry got back on its feet after the war, the front-engined coach chassis remained almost universal, and so coachbuilders revived the 'half-cab' body designs they had been building in the 1930s. This AEC Regal III with its front-entrance coach body would probably have seated between 32 and 35 passengers.

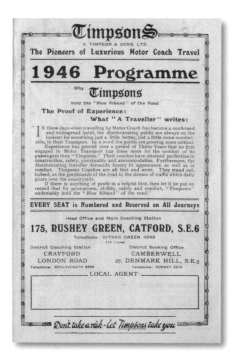

The London firm of Timpson's was quick off the mark with a coaching programme for 1946.

OPPOSITE
One of the most popular small coaches was the Bedford OB, essentially an updated pre-war design. This 1950 Duple-bodied example with 29 seats is typical.

after the hostilities were over. Many of the relatively modern express-service coaches operated by Green Line in London and the Home Counties were handed over to the American Red Cross in Britain after 1942, and were converted into mobile canteens that were known as 'clubmobiles'.

'Make do and mend' had been a catchphrase during the war years, and the coach operators had to do the same in the late 1940s. Production was geared towards export demand in order to earn revenue to help rebuild the economy; both raw materials and fuel were rationed, and austerity was the order of the day. Pre-war coaches that were long past their best were patched up and put back into revenue-earning service, and the industry was generally too busy turning out updated pre-war designs to come up with anything very new. Demand for new coaches vastly outstripped supply, and a number of new small body manufacturing companies appeared, in many cases lasting only until the boom was over.

And boom it was: the pent-up demand from customers only too keen to embrace brighter lives after the gloom of wartime ensured that there was no shortage of business for the coach operators. Some things, of course, barely changed: the annual works outing still required fleets of coaches and was still an important event in the lives of many working people in Britain. But there was also a new enthusiasm, among those who could afford such things, for holidays abroad. A sign of the times was that when Smiths Happiways of Wigan offered a 14-day coach tour to Switzerland in May 1946, it was a sell-out.

This preserved 1949 Leyland Tiger PS2 coach illustrates well the transitional style of coachwork common in the late 1940s. Although the decorative side features of this Burlingham coach body are very much in the style of the 1930s, the full front is an attempt at modernity.

While the major bus and coach operators worked flat-out to meet demand from overseas, Bedford exploited an opportunity for an affordable small coach, and their OB chassis became a huge success among smaller operators. It was a pre-war design, of which only 73 had been built before production was halted in 1939, and as re-introduced in late 1945 it often came with

Everybody's favourite seat was in the front next to the driver, and this is the driving compartment of a Bedford OB with the ubiquitous Duple Vista body.

a most attractive body by Duple that was called the Vista. This little coach had seating for up to 29 passengers, was beautifully made and equipped, and could reach 40mph – which was more than enough at a time when buses and coaches were legally limited to 30mph. The OB was a semi-forward-control design with a distinctive bull-nose front end and a gearbox whine that combined to give it a lovable character. It sold well, too: more than 12,500 had been built by the time the more modern Bedford SB replaced it in 1951 and it remains one of the most popular coaches of its time in today's preservation movement.

During the 1950s, the last decade before car ownership became widespread in Britain, coach operators catered for much the same type of demand as they had back in the 1930s. Families still visited the seaside or some other attraction by

Front-engined chassis were still in the majority for coaches by 1950, when this AEC Regal III was built. Its 32-seat coach body was built by Duple and was known as the A-type. The coach was delivered to Grey Cars, the coaching arm of Devon General, and has been preserved.

signing up for a one-day excursion run by the local coach company, and at the seaside it was commonplace to find coaches parked along the sea front where advertising boards promoted evening trips and mystery tours in the area, their smartly uniformed drivers waiting to gather names and issue tickets. There were long-distance express services too, although Britain's antiquated and congested road system meant that the term 'express' was very much a relative one. And, of course, the private-hire business was thriving for works outings, wedding parties, and other special events.

Most new coaches in the late 1940s still had their engines mounted vertically at the front, and the forward-control layout popular before the war remained common, with the driver sitting alongside the engine and a 'half-cab' front layout allowing good access to that engine for servicing. Of the major chassis makers, AEC had its Regal III, Leyland its Tiger PS1, and Crossley its SD42 range. However, the major chassis makers were already working on new ideas, and in particular at moving the engine to a position in the middle of the chassis

This remarkable coach was one of a fleet specially bodied to carry passengers from the London Air Terminal at Hammersmith to Heathrow Airport. Based on one of the original 'heavyweight' underfloor-engined chassis – an AEC Regal IV – it was new to British European Airways in 1953. The one-and-a-half deck body design, built by Park Royal, allowed a large luggage compartment at the rear.

Commer and Bedford both produced front-engined chassis suitable for full-front coachwork in the early 1950s. This is a Commer Avenger, with a 33-seat coach body by Harrington.

and under the floor where it would lie on its side. This allowed room for more passengers within the body, whose length was still limited to 27 feet 6 inches by law.

By late 1949, AEC was offering its Regal IV, and the following year Leyland introduced its Royal Tiger. Others followed, encouraged further perhaps by the relaxation of the permitted dimensions to a length of 30 feet and a width of 8 feet in 1950. The extra length allowed coach body builders to fit as many as 41 passengers into their new designs, although many chose not to go that far but to settle for more spacious accommodation and passenger seating in the high thirties.

Access to the power unit of one of these new underfloor-engined types was from underneath or through panels in the lower body sides, and so there was no need for the old half-cab designs; instead, the body makers provided full-width fronts, often with the entrance ahead of the front wheels and next to the driver. This allowed for more harmonious lines and, although some body makers indulged in flamboyant styles that failed to catch on or dated very quickly, others produced longer-lasting classics. Among these was the Burlingham Seagull, a 37-seat central-entrance design suitable for either the Regal or the Royal Tiger chassis; it was facelifted every two years or so to keep it fresh, but by the end of the 1950s was losing both its popularity and its looks.

The early underfloor-engined chassis were extremely robust and very heavy, as their makers got to grips with the new technology. By 1953, both AEC and Leyland had developed new designs of lighter weight, which were announced as the Reliance and Tiger Cub respectively. Dimensionally they were unchanged from the older designs, so the body makers were able to continue their earlier designs, but these new chassis typically weighed a ton less than their predecessors, which made for more economical running. New and lighter coach body styles began to appear to suit them, often with extensive roof glazing to give a lighter and airier interior. Typical of later 1950s styles was the Duple Britannia, still with the rotundity typical of the decade but with a much lighter appearance.

These full-front body designs quickly attracted custom, and as a result the body makers switched to full-front designs for vertical-engined chassis, too. Some older chassis were rebodied in the new style, engine access in all case being from inside the passenger saloon, where the engine was concealed under a

One of the most attractive coach bodies on early underfloor-engined chassis was the Burlingham Seagull. It evolved over the years and is seen here on a 1956 Leyland Tiger Cub chassis. The vehicle was originally operated by Ribble (based at Preston in Lancashire) on their express coach services.

Bedford's early-1950s chassis was the SB, and again Duple managed to get a large share of the body building business for it. This is a Vista coach body on a 1955 example, pictured at an enthusiasts' rally. The board displayed with it is typical of those that would have been used to attract custom when it was new.

removable cover next to the driver. Bedford did well with smaller operators, offering the front-engined SB chassis that was lighter and cheaper than the underfloor-engined types. From 1957, Ford followed suit with their Thames chassis, making sure it would take the bodies originally drawn up for the Bedford.

There were changes in the business during the late 1940s, too, as the Labour government of the day sought to bring many of the country's essential services under state control. With the Transport Act of 1947, a large part of the coaching industry was nationalised with the Tilling Group, the Red & White group, and Scottish Motor Traction. Chassis maker Bristol and body maker Eastern Coach Works went the same way, becoming dedicated suppliers of the needs of these nationalised operators, which were run by the new British Transport Commission (BTC).

One result was that although coach tours largely remained in the hands of independent

'Reliance' chassis mounted with 'Elizabethan' luxury coach body, providing seating accommodation for forty-one passengers. There is 90 cu. ft. of baggage space in the rear.

operators during the 1950s, the larger operating groups also became determined to get a share of the market. Not all were nationalised: the companies of the British Electric Traction (BET) group remained privately owned. However, their operating model was different: as bus operators, they expected a vehicle to last for 12 or 15 years before being worn out and scrapped, while the smaller companies were used to keeping up with fashion and changing their vehicles every three to five years, passing the old ones on to even smaller businesses for further use. One way the larger operators got around the problem was by calling for dual-purpose bodies, which combined the robustness (and typically the unexciting styling) of a service-bus with more comfortable seating similar to that found in coaches. The results were hardly luxurious, but they were a hard-headed approach to practicality.

By the end of the 1950s, British coach manufacture was dominated by AEC and Leyland, with Bedford and Ford catering for the smaller and lighter chassis typically demanded by independent operators. Luxury coach bodies came from Burlingham, Duple, Harrington, Plaxton and Yeates, who all built for all types of chassis. Dual-purpose bodies mostly came from the bus body builders, because they were adaptations of service-bus designs. There were around 20,000 coaches of one sort or another in service in Britain during 1958.

AEC responded to concerns about the weight of early underfloor-engined chassis with the lighter Reliance model. This one, pictured in a sales brochure with a Duple Elizabethan coach body, seated 41 passengers and also had 90 cubic feet of luggage space in the 'boot' built into the rear of the body below the seats.

OPPOSITE
The passenger's-eye view of a Duple Vista coach body, in this case on an Albion Victor rather than the more common Bedford SB chassis. Note the overhead luggage racks, the attractively patterned upholstery, the wood trim and the tinted sun panels in the roof. All were typical of the period.

Down in south-west Britain, Royal Blue (by this time part of the nationalised British Transport Commission) had a fleet of Bristol LS coaches that incorporated a rather old-fashioned looking luggage rack on the roof. One was pictured in this enticing artwork for the cover of a Royal Blue timetable.

The major design innovation towards the end of the decade came from Plaxton, whose Panorama coach body of 1958 introduced much larger windows than were usual and set a new trend. The huge glass area made the inside of these attractive coaches exceptionally light and airy, with superb visibility thanks to a reduction in the number of roof pillars – a design change that would certainly attract the attention of safety authorities today. But there were other important changes in the wind, and the most important of those was the opening of Britain's first motorways, which would provide new challenges for coach operators in the 1960s.

These were prosperous times for the coaching industry in Britain. Few Britons took holidays abroad yet, and 'the Continent' (Europe) was seen as exciting and exotic and not for the common man or woman. Car ownership was still the privilege of a minority, and Britain maintained a cosy insularity, still proud of its Commonwealth and the fact that it had 'won' the Second World War – whatever the cost.

A coach trip was still something rather special; the long-distance 'express' services might take all day (or all night) to get passengers from one end of the country to the other, and were an adventure in themselves for that reason. On-board toilets were unusual, and were found only on coaches designed specifically for these long-distance services. Among the coaches so fitted were those owned by Scottish Omnibuses and Western SMT, whose services covered around 400 miles between Scotland's major cities and London. There would usually be a driver change en route, and there would certainly be stops for refreshment as well.

Passengers board their coach for an outing in the 1950s; the trip may well have been organised by a Women's Institute or similar group.

Toilet compartments were becoming more common on coaches used for long-distance services. This one was in a 1954 Duple Ambassador body, for an AEC Reliance or Leyland Tiger Cub chassis.

Children vied with one another to occupy the rearmost seat, which would typically seat five abreast and would allow a group of friends to sit together, as well as offering the middle passenger more legroom because there was only the gangway ahead of that position. The coach driver on an excursion often found himself doubling as tour guide and chief entertainer, just as he had in the 1930s, and might get to know many of his passengers quite well during the course of a trip. On long journeys, one favourite was for the driver to run a lottery – for low stakes such as a penny per passenger. He might chalk an arrow at the top of one of the wheel arches, and then make a number of further marks on the tyre, corresponding to the number of passengers on board. When the coach stopped for a refreshment break (as much to allow the driver to recuperate as to allow the passengers access to food), the winning number was the one closest to the mark on the wheel arch, and the passenger with that number won the money.

WINDS OF CHANGE:
THE 1960s AND 1970s

T HE 1960S WAS a decade of change for the coaching industry in Britain. On the one hand, the expansion of the motorway network opened up new and exciting possibilities for coach travel, and especially for scheduled express services. On the other hand, the rise in private car ownership hit coaching revenues quite hard, as did cheaper air travel, which permitted families at all levels of the social scale to take holidays abroad. The Beeching cuts to the rail network in the early part of the decade were to some extent prompted by that same increase in private car use, and to some extent they provided opportunities for road transport

This publicity picture shows a Duple Britannia coach body on an AEC Reliance chassis, but by the time it was taken in 1960 the Britannia was already five years old and due for replacement.

The trend towards larger areas of glass is well illustrated by this 1960 Duple Super Vega coach body on a Bedford SB chassis.

operators, although probably more for rural stage-carriage services than for long-distance coach operators.

There were two Transport Acts in the 1960s, one in 1962 and the second in 1968. The main effect of the 1962 Act was on the railways but it also brought change to road transport by dissolving the British Transport Commission, which had been established in 1947. In its place came five new public corporations, each with responsibility for a sector of the transport market, and among these was the Transport Holding Company, whose assets included bus companies, road haulage companies, bus manufacturers and travel agents. Six years later, under the 1968 Act, the THC was divided into the new National Bus Company and the Scottish Transport Group (plus the National Freight Corporation).

Recognising which way the wind was blowing, the private-enterprise British Electric Traction group – some of whose constituent companies were already part-owned by the THC – sold out to the new National Bus Company as the Act was passing through Parliament. The former municipal operators were mostly merged into five regional Passenger Transport Executives (PTEs). All this left most of the industry in state ownership, and only a few operators remained independent. Among them, the largest was Yelloway Motor Services of Rochdale.

OVERLEAF
Now beautifully restored, 780 GHA is an example of BMMO's famous C5 motorway coaches. It was new in 1959 and has 37-seat coachwork by the operator.

Midland Red

780 GHA

This Duple publicity picture shows the effect of all that glass on the interior of the coach; the overhead luggage racks have steel mesh bases to ensure maximum light shines through. Note the detachable antimacassars with the initials of the coach operator.

Although there were multiple changes to the management and the running of the individual bus and coach operators now absorbed into the NBC monolith, the most obvious outward signs did not appear until 1972. That was when the NBC imposed its corporate image policy on all subsidiaries: all coaches – which were run by subsidiary National Express Coaches – would in future be painted in all-over white with the National name on the side in alternate red and blue letters, accompanied by an arrowhead logo. The name of the parent subsidiary might be found elsewhere on the vehicle in much smaller lettering, but this was no compensation for the loss of the individual liveries, whose colour and variety vanished from the coaching scene. The Scottish Bus Group, by contrast, chose to retain individual liveries despite some rebranding, and from 1976 even adopted a distinctive St Andrew's Cross logo.

Meanwhile, the spread of the motorway network prompted some far-reaching changes in coach design and also led to the opening of new long-distance services that would not have been feasible in earlier times. Using the motorways, 300 miles in a day became feasible. Coaches designed to meet the old 30mph maximum speed limit were hopelessly outdated on the motorways with their lack of speed restrictions (the 70mph limit was not introduced until 1965), and as operators called for higher cruising speeds, so the chassis makers responded with larger and more powerful engines that were able to pull the higher gearing needed for motorway use.

Two early pioneers of motorway express services were Ribble, in association with their W.C. Standerwick coaching subsidiary, and Midland Red (more formally known as BMMO and based in Smethwick, near Birmingham). The Ribble/Standerwick service from Blackpool to London via the M1 motorway opened in 1959, and nearly halved the earlier journey time. It was operated by a fleet of striking new double-deck coaches, based on the latest Leyland Atlantean chassis with air suspension on the front axle. They had coach-type seating for 50 passengers (Atlantean bus bodies seated 78), a galley and a toilet compartment; and careful use of paint and bright highlighting disguised the squareness of their Weymann bodywork.

★ Gay Hostess

RIBBLE
STANDERWICK

A new style
double-deck luxury coach
for long distance
express services

Ribble and Standerwick operated these attractive 'Gay Hostess' double-deck coaches on the Lancashire to London service via the M6 and M1 motorways.

London-based Timpson's showed one of their Harrington-bodied AEC Reliance coaches on this 1961 timetable. The visually arresting front end was made possible by the use of GRP mouldings.

They were known as Gay Hostess coaches – a name that would raise a smile today – because they carried a stewardess whose job was to provide drinks and snacks from the galley and generally to look after passengers' welfare. The original service was later extended to reach other Lancashire towns, and continued into the 1970s, the original Gay Hostess coaches giving way to a fleet of Bristol VRL double-deckers that developed a reputation for unreliability and were soon replaced by Leyland Leopard single-deckers.

Midland Red, meanwhile, made the most of their Birmingham to London service via the M1 by developing and building their own special single-deck coach. The BMMO CM5T coaches had turbo-charged engines and tall gearing, and gained a very high and glamorous profile thanks to a maximum speed of 85mph (achieved on test), and there was even a Corgi Toys model version too. The return fare for the service was just over half the train fare, there was again an on-board toilet, and the service ran three times a day. The CM5T coaches were followed by larger CM6T types in the 1960s, with a larger, non-turbo-charged engine, and the service continued successfully.

As these examples demonstrate, coach design was changing again. The 1960s had opened with some important changes in the Construction & Use Regulations, and a 36-foot overall length was permitted from 1961. This increased the seating capacity of the typical express coach from 41 (with a 30-foot overall length) to 49 or even 51 seats. At the

The Harrington Cavalier coach body, as illustrated on that 1961 Timpson's timetable, was a style leader in the early 1960s. This restored example was new to the Grey Cars coaching fleet of Devon General in 1963 and has an AEC Reliance chassis. It has 41 seats.

same time, the speed limit for PSVs on open roads was raised from the long-unenforceable 30mph to 40mph, while on the new motorways, coaches (like cars) were initially subject to no speed limit at all. An AEC Reliance with the AH590 engine (a 9.6-litre six-cylinder diesel with 153bhp) was capable of 70mph, and regularly proved it on the motorways.

the new
PLAXTONS
take a
giants step

The three-axle Bedford VAL was a popular choice in the 1960s, although it suffered from braking maladies in its early days. This is a 1965 sales brochure for the Plaxton coachwork available for the model.

The Beatles travelled in a Bedford VAL coach on their Magical Mystery Tour. This is not the original, but a replica used on tourist trips of the band's native Liverpool.

By the mid-1960s, the four most popular single-deck PSV chassis in Britain were all designed to be suitable for either bus or coach operation, the main differences lying in engine type and gearing. These were the AEC Reliance, the Leyland Leopard, the Bedford VAM and the Ford R-series; major operators tended to favour the first two, while smaller independents favoured the Bedfords and Fords. Bedford had tried hard to break the mould in 1962 with the introduction of the VAL, a three-axle coach with twin steering. The theory was that the three axles enabled the load to be spread more evenly, allowing smaller wheels which in turn permitted a lower floor height. This model also proved popular, and memorably starred in two films of the time – the Beatles' *Magical Mystery Tour* (1968) and *The Italian Job* (1969).

Air suspension became available to smooth out the ride, but coach operators approached it cautiously, fearing reliability problems. Body designs changed quite radically, new and stylish front-end designs being made possible through the increasing use of GRP mouldings. Windows became longer and deeper, making the interior of a coach more light and airy, but the preoccupation in the 1960s with plastic laminates – easier to clean than traditional wood, and cheaper, too – led to interiors that were self-consciously modern rather than luxurious in the old sense. In the era of G-Plan furniture, however, nobody complained.

There were still many important and attractive coach body designs, the very best perhaps coming from Harrington (still at Hove) and Plaxton (in Scarborough). Surprisingly, perhaps, coach body builders still tended to cater for operators in distinct regions rather than nationally; so at the start of the 1960s, Duple (in London) and Harrington sold mostly to southern fleets, while Plaxton and Burlingham (in Blackpool) were favoured by those in the north. Scottish operators found their coach bodies at Alexander (Falkirk) and those associated with the BTC

... and this is the original, with Beatle Paul McCartney standing beside the second front axle.

The interior of this 1961 Plaxton Embassy body shows the typical coach interior of the time: comfortable, but without the ostentatious luxury trappings of its 1930s equivalent.

The thrill of the coach trip: even in the 1960s, a coach trip was an exciting occasion, and this group of children was photographed before embarking on the coach that was to take them. It has another Harrington body, and the chassis is almost certainly an AEC Reliance or Leyland Leopard.

invariably had their bodies built by Eastern Coachworks (ECW) at Lowestoft before 1968.

Despite the general downturn in coaching during the 1960s, coach operators were busy, and sometimes almost frantically so. Stewart J. Brown writes in his book *Luxury Travel* of his experience working for Alexander (Midland) in Glasgow: 'On peak summer Saturdays and Sundays up to 100 vehicles would be dispatched on excursions, starting with full-day tours to far-flung destinations such as Oban and Dunoon at 8.30am, and finishing with evening mystery tours departing typically until around 6.30pm.' Demand was such that they sometimes had to schedule single-deck buses (without coach seating) or even double-deckers to do the job.

It is easy to see, then, why some of the major operators favoured dual-purpose coachwork so that a vehicle could

Duple developed its rounded designs of the 1950s into squarer shapes to suit the tastes of the 1960s. This is a Bella Vega design on a 1965 Bedford SB belonging to Ingatestone Coaches, a small Essex independent operator. The bright wheel trims were typical of the accessories favoured by such companies.

be used for bus work when it was not required for express service work – and vice versa (see page 35). This of course meant that, during the 1960s, those who travelled on the express services operated by the larger companies quite often travelled in rather less luxury than those who travelled with the smaller independents.

The 1970s turned out to be a troubling decade for the coaching industry in Britain, and the submersion of individual operating identities into the National Bus Company was

Plaxton coachwork was very distinctive in the 1960s and early 1970s, featuring huge side windows. Not for nothing was this style known as the Panorama. This 1971 example on a 39-foot AEC Reliance chassis was new to East Kent.

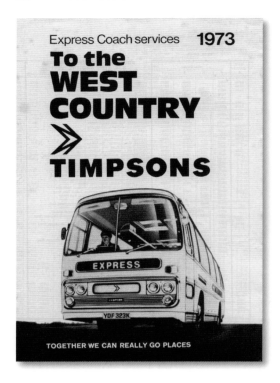

Express Coach services **1973**

To the
WEST
COUNTRY

≫

TIMPSONS

EXPRESS

YDF 323K

TOGETHER WE CAN REALLY GO PLACES

That front-end design, though subtly different on this later example, was readily recognisable as belonging to a Plaxton body. In this case, it provides the illustration for a 1973 timetable for Timpson's express coach services between London and the West Country.

only a small part of this. The 1970s was a decade of industrial unrest, and this inevitably affected the motor industry. There were several effects; most troubling of all, perhaps, was that British-built vehicles earned a reputation for unreliability (mostly the result of poor build quality), and this was compounded by difficulties in spares supply. The one thing that no coach operator can tolerate is a vehicle that is off the road for lack of spare parts to repair it, and as a result many began to look outside Britain for new vehicles.

All this in turn had its effect on the manufacturing side of the business. Chassis maker AEC, which had merged with Leyland in 1962, closed down in 1979. Several of the coach body builders disappeared. Duple closed its London headquarters in 1968 and relocated to Blackpool and the premises of its Duple (Northern) subsidiary, which had once been Burlingham. Harrington had built its last coach bodies in 1966, passing the design rights for its bodies to Plaxton. Plaxton, sensibly, saw what was happening and began in 1976 to follow continental European design trends with the high-floor Viewmaster coach body (with luggage room under the floor). It was one of the few companies to survive.

When Britain's coach operators turned to continental European manufacturers for their new vehicles, the whole look of the country's coaching operations changed. The high-floor European-style coach body was much taller than the traditional British single-decker, and continental trends in

Plaxton had some attractive designs for the smaller coach chassis, too. This one is an Embassy style on a 1964 Bedford VAS chassis. Once again, the large glass area is evident.

the 1970s were towards square-rigged designs rather than the more graceful styles favoured in Britain. Yet the continental European chassis designs did have the important reliability factor. While the state-owned operators of the National Bus Company tended to stay with British chassis as a matter of policy, the smaller independents increasingly bought from Mercedes-Benz in Germany, from DAF in the Netherlands, or from Volvo in Sweden.

Duple had no choice but to copy the large-window style of the Plaxton Panorama, although there were distinct differences. This is a 1978 example on a Ford R1114 chassis for Wells Continental Coaches of Maldon in Essex.

MODERN TIMES

EVEN THOUGH MANY of the developments of the 1960s and 1970s seemed exciting, it soon became clear that the future for coach services was not promising. It was true that the motorways made long-distance express services much faster than they had ever been before, but it was also true that more and more people preferred to travel along them by car. Car travel also dealt some serious blows to the market for coach excursions, offering greater flexibility and convenience than coach operators could ever achieve.

Then there were changes in the holiday preferences of the average Briton. Touring holidays, with a stop at a different hotel every night, went out of fashion. Instead, people wanted to go to one place and stay there for a week, or maybe two if they could afford the cost and the time off work. Above all, cheaper air travel promised holiday locations with guaranteed good weather.

Yet long-distance express services remained an important element in coach travel. The motorway network was by this stage fundamental to the network of services that had grown up, and an inevitable development was a new type of coach station, situated just off the motorway so that express coaches did not have to waste time or create congestion by driving into major towns. These were called coachway interchanges, and the first one was built just off the M1 motorway near Milton Keynes in 1989. Passengers wishing to join one of the express services that stopped there could get access by using

park-and-ride services or other local bus services from nearby towns. Other coachway interchanges were subsequently created near Sheffield, Portsmouth, High Wycombe and in southern Fife.

Despite such developments, and despite developments in the coaches themselves that made coach travel a far more pleasant experience than it had ever been, long-distance coach travel continued to decline after the 1990s. One reason was of course the increasing congestion on Britain's roads, which contributed to extended (and sometimes unpredictable) journey times. Although coach travel generally remained cheaper than the rail alternative in the modern era, quicker travel by rail proved to be a decisive advantage. After 1996, a new franchising system for rail passenger services led to keener pricing and (to some extent) better service schedules, and the decline in coach use was then matched by a marked growth in use of the railways. Ironically, perhaps, five of the original railway franchises went to National Express, the state-owned coach operator.

Tour and excursion advertising remained familiar. This was the view outside the offices of Caroline Seagull, coach operators at Great Yarmouth.

The 'bus' branding is misleading, but the Megabus operation would once have been described as an express coach service.

Political and legislative changes made their own contribution to change in this period. The Thatcher government, elected in 1979, was hell-bent on increasing private ownership and stimulating business through competition. An early piece of legislation was the Transport Act of 1980, which removed express coach services of longer than 35 miles from the regulation system that then allocated certain routes to certain operators and denied others the opportunity to compete for business.

'Deregulation', as it was called, led to a brief revitalisation of express coach services, as new operators seized their chance to grab a piece of the market. On the very day it came into force, a consortium of established operators calling itself British Coachways started a series of services with the aim of undermining the dominance of National Express. But their challenge was short-lived: the member companies were forced to charge very low fares to attract custom from the existing carrier, and found profit margins too slim to be viable. One by one, they withdrew from the alliance, which folded completely in 1982. Competition nevertheless remained fierce in some areas, and a notable example was the Oxford to London service, where Stagecoach Oxfordshire and the Oxford Bus Company each fought their corner for business. The Newcastle to London service attracted no fewer than three operators during 1984, as Armstrong Galley, Blueline, and Rapide coaches vied for shares of a lucrative route.

Competition, plus that gradually falling demand for coach services, led to rapid and sometimes dramatic changes among the coach operators themselves. New liveries accompanied the arrival of each new operator, adding to the colour of the coaching scene although certainly not reducing its complication. The National Express franchise operation, formerly state owned, was privatised in a management buyout during 1988, and in 1993 it took over Scottish CityLink, a similar operation formed in 1985 in Scotland and similarly sold to its own management, in this case in 1990. National Express then fell foul of the Competition Commission and was obliged to sell Scottish CityLink again in 1998.

Another new challenge entered the arena in 2003, when Stagecoach launched its Megabus operation in England and Scotland, increasing competition in the business and leading to some lowering of fares. But when it established a joint venture with ComfortDelGro (who had bought Scottish CityLink), the Competition Commission again intervened and in 2008 Stagecoach sold some of its services. More competition arrived in 2009 when First Group entered the market with Greyhound UK (named after the well-known transcontinental bus company in the USA), competing with both Megabus and National Express, but the company closed its services in December 2015.

Inevitably, there were other legislative changes that affected coach services in this period. Speed limiters were introduced for coaches in 1988, initially set at 70mph (the national

The Volvo B10M became very popular in the 1980s and, in this case, carried bodywork by the British coachbuilder Duple.

The major British coach manufacturer of recent times has been Dennis, and this 1990 Javelin model carries a body by a British company too – in this case, Duple.

motorway limit) but reduced to 65mph in 1994. Coaches were increasingly capable of maintaining high motorway speeds, and from the start of 2008 they were banned from the third line of motorways by law, preventing them from blocking faster traffic. Seat belts became mandatory in all new coaches, and from 2006 the law required all passengers over the age of three to wear a belt if one was available.

Very noticeable from the late 1970s onwards was that British coach manufacturers themselves began to change. The leading makers of coach chassis had for many years been AEC and Leyland, although Leyland had owned both marques since 1962. Leyland's acquisition of the major players in the British car industry (at government behest) ultimately led to its collapse and nationalisation in 1975. AEC closed its doors in 1979 and then the Leyland bus and coach business was sold to its managers in 1987. A year later, those managers sold it to Volvo – the major Swedish maker of buses and coaches. As a badge on British coaches, Leyland had disappeared within five years.

Only Dennis survived as a major force in the business, re-emerging in the 1970s after pulling out of the PSV market during the previous decade. A complex set of ownership

Typical of the early European imports is this 1981 Setra 215HD, with rear engine, high floor level and integral (chassisless) construction.

German manufacturer Neoplan specialised in spectacular-looking designs. This 1983 Skyliner is a three-axle double-deck coach with a 40-foot overall length, and was operated by Trathens Travel Services of Plymouth.

changes over the next three decades saw it become Alexander Dennis in 2004, by then incorporating some of the old and respected names among coach body builders – notably Alexander in Scotland and Plaxton in Scarborough. Alexander Dennis has gone on to become Britain's biggest maker of PSVs, notable designs being the Javelin coach chassis (1986–2010) and the R series rear-engined coach chassis from 1999.

Not surprisingly, other makers moved into the market to take advantage of this disarray within the British industry. Those makers were all from the European continent or Scandinavia, and new names entered the British coaching business. From Germany came Kässbohrer-Setra (usually badged Setra) and Neoplan, whose futuristic coach designs proved attractive to many of the new operators who were trying to get a foothold in the market after deregulation. In later years, both companies would be absorbed by other

Victoria Coach
Station in
London remains
an important
focus of coaching
activity in the
city. Only the
vehicles have
changed over
the years, as this
2010 picture
shows. Note
the destination
board reading
'London–Oxford
in style'!

German PSV makers. Setra went to Mercedes-Benz in 1995, and Neoplan to MAN in 2001.

Mercedes-Benz had already gained customers for its O350 range, and MAN made headway by developing integral-construction models with leading coach body builders. From Sweden, Scania also gained customers by supplying the mechanical units that other companies built into complete vehicles. Volvo's B10M chassis secured a large share of the market, too. Built between 1978 and 2003, this had its engine mounted under the floor at the rear, and from 1990 it was even built in Britain for both domestic and export customers – at the former Leyland Bus plant in Workington, Cumbria. The B10M was replaced by the B12 and other models that maintained strong sales for Volvo in the coach market.

These imported chassis brought some important changes to the coaches sold in Britain. They had been

developed for countries where coaching conditions were rather different from those in Britain, with sustained high-speed travel on motorways and longer distances being commonplace requirements. As a result, they generally had more powerful engines than their British predecessors. Air suspension

became the new standard to give a more comfortable ride. Although some of these coaches were bodied by the remaining British coach body builders, many came with bodies that were also built abroad. Body specifications became ever more luxurious – although the luxury was most perceptible in levels of equipment and not in the way that British coaches of the 1930s had been luxurious.

The shape of the modern coach is represented here by Irizar, a Spanish builder, on a 2012 Scania chassis from Sweden.

So it was not surprising that coach body builders from the European continent soon began to dominate the coaching scene in Britain. Of the four major players, only Irizar was based in Spain, and it built coach bodies on MAN, Mercedes-Benz and Volvo chassis, as well as creating integral coaches jointly with Scania. The other three were Berkhof (in the Netherlands), Bova (also in the Netherlands, and specialising in integral construction), and Jonckheere (in Belgium). Amalgamations and takeovers from the late 1990s saw all three of them in the ownership of the VDL Group before 2004, and the suppression of the individual makers' names after 2010.

The Jonckheere body on this 1997 Volvo B10M has a typical curved front profile, high floor and huge rear-view mirrors.

Coach body design changed fundamentally towards the end

The coachwork here is by Jonckheere again, with the later front end design incorporating small round lights. This is again a Volvo chassis, this time from 2003, and was operated by FirstGroup of Aberdeen.

Those characteristic rear-view mirrors were incorporated into the coach graphic used on coach stops such as this one in Brighton.

of the century, too. The typical design now had a raised floor level, the high-set seating providing a better all-round view through panoramic windows and the space below being reserved for passengers' luggage. Amenities gradually increased to meet customer expectations and to offer a more luxurious coaching experience, making the modern coach quite different from its 'classic' mid-century counterpart. Air conditioning became common, together with panoramic windows, an on-board toilet, and free Wi-Fi. Seat design drew on aircraft practice, and in many cases incorporated multi-way adjustment

and perhaps a tray with a drinks holder as well. In the early years of the twenty-first century, many new coaches were ordered with a TV screen for each seat that gave access to TV, music and games.

Despite all the challenges, coach travel in Britain is holding its own. There is still a demand for mystery tours

This striking Neoplan Tourliner N2216SHD coach was new to Lakeside Coaches of Ellesmere in the Lake District.

and excursions, typically from retired people, although it is not what it once was. School excursion work keeps some operators busy. The demand for express coach services continues too, in particular those that allow commuting in relative comfort from an outlying town into a larger city; anyone who has

Neoplan's Starliner coach was another arresting design. This 2013 example belonged to Edwards Coaches of Llantwit Fardre, then the largest holiday coach operator in Wales. It is pictured at Weymouth.

This 2016 Volvo B11RT was new to Selwyns Travel of Runcorn, who operated it on behalf of National Express. The body is a Portuguese-built Caetano Levante, available for chassis with either two or three axles. It incorporates a front-mounted lift to enable wheelchair passengers to board through the front door.

regularly commuted by train in such circumstances will know the discomfort and disadvantages associated with it. There is also still a demand for coaches to carry parties of VIPs, or simply wedding and other parties, for relatively short distances and between points that cannot be connected by train. For the foreseeable future, the coach will remain in demand.

One problem that continues to confront coach operators is the impact of clean-air legislation. Some British cities have introduced ULEZ zones (the letters stand for Ultra-Low Emissions Zone), which means that operators who wish to run coaches into them must either buy new vehicles that meet the relevant standards or upgrade older ones where the option exists. In the longer term, this may well have an effect on the business model that many fleets have used, as it could seriously undermine the second-hand value of vehicles in their fleets. Perhaps the future will lie with leasing rather than ownership of coaches, transferring the financial risk to the leasing company. Whatever the outcome, Britain's coach operators are certain to find a way of maintaining that long and, at times, glorious tradition of coaching.

FURTHER READING

Brown, Stewart J. *Luxury Travel: Coach Designs in Britain, 1958–73*. Capital Transport, 1998.

Deegan, Peter and Deegan, Judith A. *Standerwick & Scout*. Venture Publications, 1994.

Lockwood, Stan. *Kaleidoscope of Char-a-bancs and Coaches*. Marshall, Harris & Baldwin Ltd, 1980.

McLachlan, Tom. *Grey-Green and Contemporaries, Book One (to 1960)*. Arthur Southern Ltd, 2007.

PLACES TO VISIT

Some of these museums host running days, when vintage coaches from their collections or in private ownership provide rides in the local area.

British Commercial Vehicle Museum, King Street, Leyland, Lancashire PR25 2LE. Telephone: 01772 451011. Website: www.britishcommercialvehiclemuseum.com

Isle of Wight Bus & Coach Museum, The Bus Depot, Park Road, Ryde, Isle of Wight PO33 2BE. Telephone: 01983 567796. Website: www.iwbusmuseum.org.uk

London Bus Museum, Cobham Hall, Brooklands Road, Weybridge KT13 0QS. Telephone: 01932 837994. Website: www.londonbusmuseum.com

Oxford Bus Museum, Hanborough Rail Station Yard, Main Road, Long Hanborough, Woodstock OX29 8LA. Telephone: 01993 883617 (when the Museum is open), or 01296 337622 (when closed). Website: www.oxfordbusmuseum.org

Scottish Vintage Bus Museum, M90 Commerce Park, Dunfermline KY12 0SJ. Telephone: 01383 623380. Website: www.svbm.online

INDEX